CODING

Angie Smibert and Alexis Roumanis

AV² provides enriched content that supplements and complements this book. Weigl's AV² books strive to create inspired learning and engage young minds in a total learning experience.

Your AV² Media Enhanced books come alive with...

Audio
Listen to sections of the book read aloud.

Key Words
Study vocabulary, and complete a matching word activity.

Video
Watch informative video clips.

Quizzes
Test your knowledge.

Embedded Weblinks
Gain additional information for research.

Slide Show
View images and captions, and prepare a presentation.

Try This!
Complete activities and hands-on experiments.

... and much, much more!

Go to www.av2books.com, and enter this book's unique code.

BOOK CODE

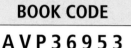

AVP36953

AV² by Weigl brings you media enhanced books that support active learning.

Published by AV² by Weigl
350 5th Avenue, 59th Floor
New York, NY 10118
Website: www.av2books.com

Library of Congress Control Number: 2017962137

ISBN 978-1-4896-7574-3 (hardcover)
ISBN 978-1-4896-7911-6 (softcover)
ISBN 978-1-4896-7575-0 (multi-user eBook)

Printed in the United States of America in Brainerd, Minnesota
1 2 3 4 5 6 7 8 9 0   22 21 20 19 18

042018
120817

Project Coordinator: Jared Siemens   Designer: Ana María Vidal

First Published by North Star Editions in 2017

Content Consultant: Jeffrey Miller, Associate Professor of Engineering Practice, Department of Computer Science, University of Southern California

pe>
_ open 09
_opr 88

rate

current system//

update 5311245109941; document current
{ >td class = mute styls backgroud compose aj; a1152615 p 22

";"process" OSSICW (page) width :33120 ca packing

HTML; = def" so= MM >> cx

{ </tr> !
{Tab>> Os aw ar j= 0:{ }
>{ </div> OSS
ossicc d.MM (
n>>>
r : byte [11024] ; s
{ tab comman
{ LIB FLANE F
nfig = manager C
efcon rc 6624<{P6
ss orsaa local 1

Contents

⌨ Code Club International is a volunteer-led coding club for kids age 9 to 13. They have more than 10,000 clubs in 12 different countries.

Your First Code

The bell rings, and you rush to coding club. You are excited to continue working on your video game. In the game, a queen has to find her way through a maze. On one side of your screen, you see the maze and the character you made. On the other side is a white space.

n the middle of your monitor are colored blocks with commands on them. These blocks will make the queen move. You drag a block to the white space. The command on the block says `WHEN RUN`. You drop more blocks underneath it. They say `MOVE FORWARD`, `TURN RIGHT`, and `MOVE FORWARD`. When you click the run button, your hero moves forward, turns right, and moves forward again. Your code is working!

⌨ Colored text used in code is called syntax highlighting. Different categories of code are visually distinct to make it easier for people to write code.

Visual coding languages are easy and fun ways to learn coding. A code, or program, is simply a set of instructions telling the computer what to do. Coding is the act of writing those instructions.

Coding has been around longer than computers themselves. Ada Lovelace wrote the first code in 1843 for a computer that existed only on paper. She showed how the computer could be programmed to do complex calculations. The principles of Ada's code are still used in computer programming today.

Ada Lovelace studied advanced mathematics and was fascinated by the inner workings of machinery.

The first computers were not built until the 1930s. A computer called Colossus was designed during World War II (1939–1945). But Colossus did not have a written code to tell it what to do. Instead, its programmers had to set the computer's plugs and switches in a new position every time the computer ran.

Colossus helped the British decipher coded messages sent by the German military during World War II. Today, Colossus is held at the National Museum of Computing in Bletchley, England.

Programmers soon realized they needed an easier way to give computers instructions. One of the first programming languages, FORTRAN, was invented in the 1950s. Other languages soon followed.

Since then, both computers and code have evolved. Now computers are everywhere. They are found on desks and laps. People carry them in their pockets. Some people even have computers in their bodies to help with health problems. All of these devices run on code.

Artificial hearts run on code. An artificial heart must beat about **100,000 times** every **24 hours** to be effective.

More than **75 percent** of Americans own a desktop or laptop computer.

Chapter 2

⌨ Scratch is a programming language that was developed by the Massachusetts Institute of Technology (MIT) to help children learn code. The programming language allows users to easily drag and drop colored blocks of code.

How Coding Works

Computers need specific instructions to do anything. A program is a set of instructions a computer follows. Coders use a variety of programming languages. These include Scratch, JavaScript, C, Ruby, and many more.

However, computers do not understand programming languages without help. The code needs to be translated into the computer's native language, called machine code. The most basic instructions are called **binary**. It is a language made up of zeros and ones. Each digit tells a tiny switch in the computer to be off or on. To tell a computer to do something, coders need to flip these switches in different combinations.

```
101010010001010101010010101010101011
101101011010111010101110101001000
010010101010101011101010110101101
101011101010010001010101010010101010
111010101101011010111010101110101
0101010100101010101011101010110
```

All high-level programming languages are translated into machine codes, such as binary.

Translators

Programming languages differ in how they are translated into machine code. An interpreter translates the code line by line as the program runs. This makes it easy for coders to find errors. A compiler translates the whole program into machine code before it runs. The machine code is then stored and saved separately from the source code.

Machine code is difficult for humans to read. Plus, each computer has millions of switches. That is why most coders use high-level programming languages. These languages are written in commands that are closer to human language.

arg in sys.argv
try:
(arg, 'r'
exp = mor
'cannot ope

Successful coders often break problems into smaller steps. Sometimes, writing down these steps is a helpful way to group different sections of code.

Thinking Like a Coder

The hardest part about coding is not learning a programming language. The hardest part is learning to explain ideas to a machine. Computers cannot guess what you mean. All of the steps need to be broken down into smaller chunks so the computer can follow them.

Events drive many codes. The code tells the computer how to handle an event such as a mouse click or key press. An if-then statement tells the computer what to do if something happens.

Loops

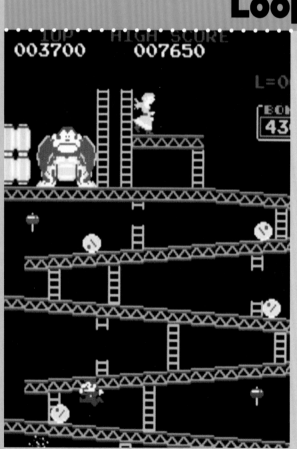

Coders do not like to type the same command over and over again. They use **loops**. A loop is part of the code that repeats itself. For instance, if you want the character to move forward 10 times, you do not have to type the same command 10 times. You simply set up a loop, and the computer runs through the command 10 times. In the 1981 arcade game Donkey Kong, a loop occurs each time a barrel is thrown. You can also use loops with if-then statements.

For example, when you test out your code, you might notice a small problem. Your character moves through the walls of your maze. You have not told the computer what to do if the character runs into something. To fix this problem, you could write an if-then statement. In Scratch, the command might look like the following.

```
If touching color blue, then
Move -2 steps
```

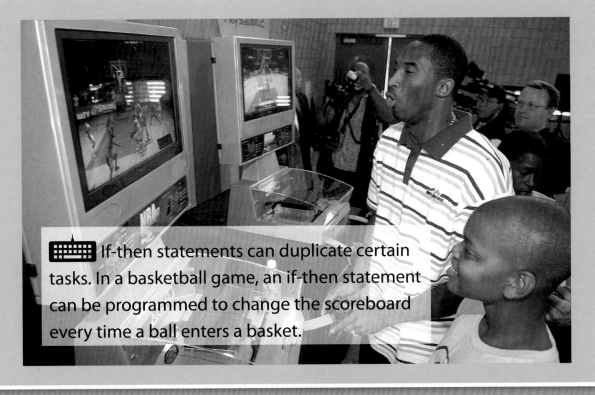

⌨ If-then statements can duplicate certain tasks. In a basketball game, an if-then statement can be programmed to change the scoreboard every time a ball enters a basket.

Programming an Event

Imagine you want your character to move when you click an arrow key. First, you must tell the computer how to react when an arrow key is clicked. You might start by writing it out in English.

When the left arrow key is pressed, point the character left and move 10 steps.

In Scratch, directions are spelled out in degrees. So, zero degrees is up, 90 degrees is right, 180 degrees is down, and 270 degrees is left. In Scratch, the command might look like the following.

```
When left arrow key pressed
Point in direction 270
Move 10 steps
```

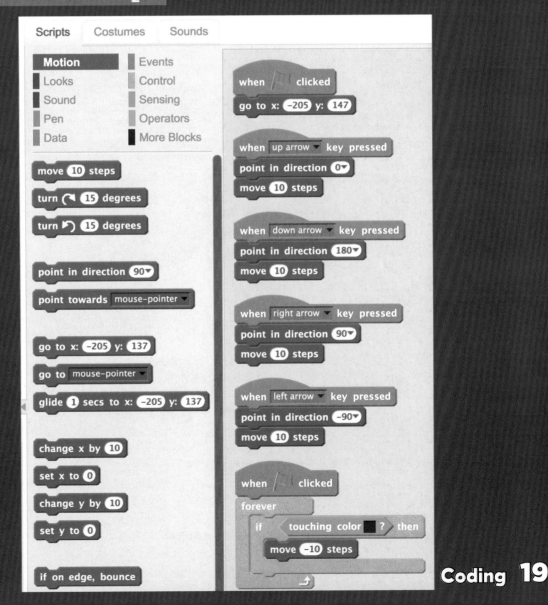

Chapter 4

Countries Affected by WannaCry 2.0 Ransomware Attack

United Kingdom
48 Hospitals and
several surgeries
impacted.

Russia
Central bank, state railway
company, major
telecommunications firm
impacted.

United States
Major shipping company
affected.

● Affected by WannaCry 2.0

🏳 Flags: Individual exam...

⌨ In 2017, a malware called WannaCry infected more than 200,000 computers around the world. People were locked out of their computers unless they paid a fee.

THE WHITE
WASHING

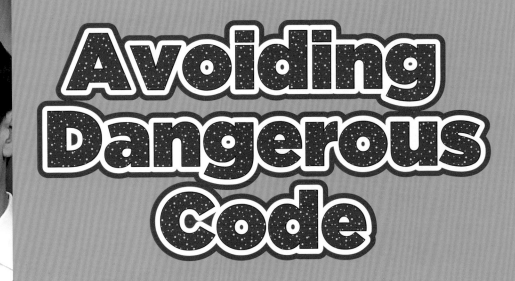

Avoiding Dangerous Code

Like any tool, code can be used for destructive as well as creative purposes. Some people write code to attack computers, steal information , or spy on people. This type of code is called malware. Malware can include **viruses**, **worms**, **adware**, and **spyware**.

HOUSE

N

⌨ Bitdefender is a popular freeware antivirus software that people can use to protect their machines from all kinds of malware.

Viruses and worms are programs that can infect your device. A virus may be attached to an e-mail or downloaded from a website. When you click on the affected file, the virus's code runs. Its code might tell it to damage the device. A worm is similar to a virus. However, it does not require the user to click on the file.

Adware and spyware are programs that run in the background. Adware typically displays advertising when you are online. Spyware is a program that has been downloaded without your permission. Spyware secretly tracks your activities on your device.

How do you protect yourself from dangerous code? First, do not click on suspicious files or links from strangers. Second, use antivirus and antimalware **software** to protect your device.

About **8 million** households in the United States have **spyware** problems each year.

Malware costs U.S. households about **$4.55 billion** each year.

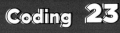

Chapter 5

Google's self-driving cars use code to determine routes and to process the information that their sensors gather.

The Future of Code

Today, more and more devices are connected to the internet and to each other. It is already possible to start a car or turn on the lights at home with a **smartphone**. The car and the lights are connected to the internet through code.

More than five billion things are connected to the internet. In the future, nearly every object might be connected through the Internet of Things. This is a network of devices, machines, objects, and even people. They can share data with each other without much human interaction.

Smartshoes are connected to the Internet of Things. They can track a user's steps, distance traveled, and speed.

⌨ Engineers are working on fridges that are connected to the Internet of Things. Interior sensors may be capable of ordering a carton of milk when the old one is empty.

Each "thing" on the Internet of Things network would have a built-in sensor. For instance, the sensors in a car might be connected to the traffic system that monitors the roads. If an accident happens, the traffic system could tell your car to take a detour to avoid the accident.

In the past, coding has been about telling computers exactly what to do. These days, programmers are using code to help computers learn from experience. For instance, Netflix has a programming code that learns which kinds of movies you like. They do this by keeping track of what you watch.

Biological Computing

Another exciting area for coders is biology. In the 1990s, scientists showed how **DNA** can be used to solve certain mathematical problems. Today, scientists are using DNA to store and recall data. Someday they may be able to program complex codes in living cells.

In 2016, Google's AlphaGo supercomputer took on professional Go players at the Google DeepMind Challenge Match in South Korea.

Google's supercomputer learned to beat human players at a board game called Go. The game is complex, making Go a good test for machine learning. The coders programmed the computer to learn. This is called machine learning. The computer learned by playing the game against itself millions of times. Computers still need code, but they will use those instructions, much like humans do, to learn from experience.

1 Who wrote the first code in 1843 for a computer that existed only on paper?

2 What helped the British decipher coded messages sent by the German military during World War II?

3 What is the name of the basic language of instructions that is made up of zeros and ones?

4 What is a part of a code that repeats itself called?

5 What type of malware secretly tracks activities on your device?

6 What is the network of devices, machines, objects, and even people called?

```
1   <!DOCTYPE html>
2   <html lang="en-us">
3       <head>
4           <title>pagename</title>
5           <meta name="Author" content="author">
6           <meta name="Description" content="description">
7           <meta name="Keywords" content="keywords">
8           <meta charset="utf-8">
9           <link rel="icon" type="image/icon" href="favicon.ico">
10          <link rel="stylesheet" type="text/css" href="style.css">
11          <style>
12              reset              { margin:0; padding:0; }
13              .clear             { clear:both; }
14              .cleared:after     { content:"."; display:block; height:0; clear:both; }
15              .right             { float:right; }
16              .left              { float:left; }
17              a img              { border:0; }
18              img                { max-width:100%; }
19              header, footer     { display:block; }
20              body               { margin:0;padding:0; }
21          </style>
22          <script src="script.js"></script>
23          <script>
24              $(document).ready(function(){
```

Answers

1. Ada Lovelace **2.** A computer called Colossus **3.** Binary
4. A loop **5.** Spyware **6.** The Internet of Things

Key Words

adware: software that generates online advertisements on a device

binary: consisting of two parts; a method for representing information by using the numbers zero and one

DNA: the genetic material in the cells of living organisms

events: actions that a computer recognizes

loops: series of instructions that are repeated in a computer program until a specified condition is met

smartphone: a mobile phone that does many of the same functions as a computer

software: the programs that run on a computer and perform certain functions

spyware: software that allows someone to track another's computer activities

viruses: programs that are designed to harm a computer and can be spread secretly from one computer to another

worms: malware programs that cause damage to computers connected to each other by a network

Index

Log on to www.av2books.com

AV² by Weigl brings you media enhanced books that support active learning. Go to www.av2books.com, and enter the special code found on page 2 of this book. You will gain access to enriched and enhanced content that supplements and complements this book. Content includes video, audio, weblinks, quizzes, a slide show, and activities.

AV² Online Navigation

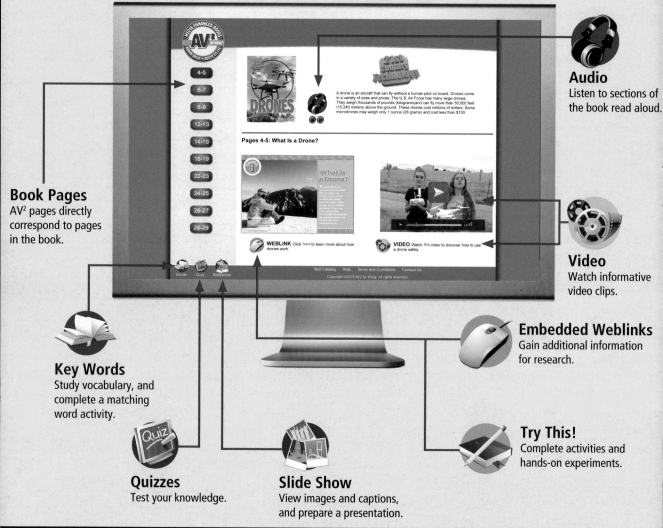

Book Pages
AV² pages directly correspond to pages in the book.

Key Words
Study vocabulary, and complete a matching word activity.

Quizzes
Test your knowledge.

Slide Show
View images and captions, and prepare a presentation.

Audio
Listen to sections of the book read aloud.

Video
Watch informative video clips.

Embedded Weblinks
Gain additional information for research.

Try This!
Complete activities and hands-on experiments.

AV² was built to bridge the gap between print and digital. We encourage you to tell us what you like and what you want to see in the future.

Sign up to be an AV² Ambassador at www.av2books.com/ambassador.